1850 and 1860

An Amherst County Index
To
The U.S. Slave Schedule

II

VIRGINIA
1850 and 1860

An
Amherst County Index
to the
U.S. Slave Schedule

Compiled and Transcribed by
Tyrone Brown

HERITAGE BOOKS
2011

HERITAGE BOOKS

AN IMPRINT OF HERITAGE BOOKS, INC.

Books, CDs, and more—Worldwide

For our listing of thousands of titles see our website
at
www.HeritageBooks.com

Published 2011 by
HERITAGE BOOKS, INC.
Publishing Division
100 Railroad Ave. #104
Westminster, Maryland 21157

International Standard Book Numbers
Paperbound: 978-0-7884-5276-5
Clothbound: 978-0-7884-8603-6

Dedication

In memory of all the ancestors of Amherst County, Virginia, especially the Slaves, the search for whom inspirited me to creation this index, I respectfully dedicate this book.

Contents

VIII

Preface

The idea to make this personal index available to the general public and genealogical community sprang from several visits to the National Archives-Mid Atlantic Region (Center City Philadelphia). Some visitors were having difficulty locating surnames in the U. S. Federal Slave Schedules. The sounds of frustration were amusing at first. Having gone through the U.S. Federal Slave Schedules many times, I offered my services and notes to a few researchers. We got satisfying results.

I hope this index is as instrumental to all who open its covers, as it is for me in quickly locating surnames and slaves in the Amherst County, Virginia, Federal slave schedules of 1850 and 1860. Thanks for purchasing this book.

Introduction

This index was created out of the necessity for a more efficient method of finding slave owners in the Amherst County, Virginia slave schedules of 1850 and 1860. It covers seven-hundred and one entries for slave owners in alphabetical order for 1860 and five-hundred and ninety-one entries for 1850.

The census taker for the 1850 Amherst County Slave Schedule was Richard Powell. His enumeration dates were August 28, 1850 to December 24, 1850. He also covered the same district for the regular census. The Amherst County slave count in 1850 was 2,981 males and 2,972 females for a total of 5,953 slaves. 12,699 was the total population count.

The enumerator and assistant marshal for the 1860 Amherst County Slave Schedule was James A. Higginbotham. He started on June 11th in the Eastern District of Amherst County, and finished November 6th 1860. Higginbotham also enumerated the free census for this same area. In 1860, the count of slaves in Amherst County was 3,240 males and 3,038 females bringing the total to 6,278 slaves. The total population count was 13,742.

There are nine columns of information for the 1850 index and ten columns for 1860 index. The first column is the numerical order. The second column lists the slave owners or employers. Column three records the number of slaves owned. For columns four and five, the amounts of male and female slaves are shown. The sixth and seventh columns reflect the number of black and mulatto slaves. The eighth column makes note of slaves who were deaf, dumb, blind, insane, or idiotic. The microfilm page number is located in the ninth column of the 1850 index, whereas; the number of slave houses is listed in column nine of the 1860 index. The tenth column for the 1860 index is the microfilm page reference number. Lastly, fugitives of the state are registered in the tenth column of the actual census record. For this index, I use page reference number/s to locate the pages where a slave owner is recorded in the slave schedule. Not listed in this index are the ages of the slaves. See the actual slave schedules for information about neighbors and ages of slaves, which are listed generally from oldest to youngest.

Some of the slaves had special skills and were hired out to other slave owners/employers (e.g. farmers, planters, the county, etc.) as masons, carpenters, blacksmiths, or breeders.

Two additional sections on overseers and slaves who have reached their centennial years have been added for 1860 and 1850.

I created an Enumeration Calendar for 1850. This calendar helps users understand that some of the material recorded is out of chronological or page order.

1850-List of slaves 100 years and older in the Amherst County slave Schedule.

1-_____, unnamed black woman, 100yrs. enumerated with *Elizabeth Camm*#52, on page 741.

2-_____, unnamed black woman, 100yrs. enumerated with *Sarah A. Waller*#532, on page 795.

3-_____, unnamed black woman, 100yrs. enumerated with *Elijah Fletcher*#148, on page 795 and 795b.

4-_____, unnamed black woman, 110yrs. enumerated with Mary Mundy#322, on page 785b.

5-_____, unnamed black woman, 100yrs. enumerated with Catherine Watts#540, on page 729b.

6-_____, unnamed black woman, 100yrs. enumeration with Richard G. Morris#316, on page 765b.

1

2

Description of 1850 Columns

1. Column#1-the numerical order of entries.
2. Column#2-the surname of slave owners in alphabetical order.
3. Column#3-(S) indicates the number of slave owned.
4. Column#4-(M) indicates the number of male slaves.
5. Column#5-(F) indicates the number of female slaves.
6. Column#6-(B) indicates the number of slaves considered black.
7. Column#7-(Mu) indicates the number of slaves considered mulatto.
8. Column#8-(X) represents the number of slaves who might be deaf and dumb, insane or idiotic. Check the original census record for specifics.
9. Column#9-page reference numbers where slave owner entries can be found in the original 1850 microfilm of Amherst County Slave Schedule.

Note- See the 1850 Slave Schedule for specifics about column eight. Not all these slave owners owned slaves but rented, borrowed, or held them in trust for legal reasons. Some free blacks and Native Americans owned family members. I found many spelling variations in the slave schedules, the 1850 regular census, and the 1850 Amherst County, Virginia Index of the regular census, published by Accelerated indexing system, Inc. 1976.

4

Enumeration Calendar

Below is the chronological order of enumeration in the eastern district of 1850 Amherst County with corresponding page numbers. If there is a (b) after a page number, look to the next page after the number. There is no letter (b) in the 1850 Slave Schedule. I chose this method because every other page is numbered. These numbers are handwritten with a dark marker at the top of the Slave Schedule pages.

	Enumeration Calendar	1850 Slave Schedule
1.	August 28th	p.656, p. 657
2.	September 9th	p. 657b
3.	September 10th	p. 661
4.	September 14th	p. 661b
5.	September 21st	p. 665
6.	September 25th	p. 665b
7.	September 28th	p. 669, p. 669b
8.	September 30th	p. 673
9.	October 4th	p. 673b, 677
10.	October 8th	p. 677b, 681
11.	October 11th	p. 681b
12.	October 12th	p. 685
13.	October 15th	p. 685b
14.	October 16th	p. 689
15.	October 19th	p. 689b
16.	October 21st	p. 693
17.	October 22nd	p. 693b, p. 697
18.	October 25th	p. 697b

	Enumeration Calendar	1850 Slave Schedule
19.	October 26th	p. 701
20.	October 28th	p. 701b, p. 705
21.	October 29th	p. 705b
22.	October 30th	p. 709
23.	November 1st	p. 709b, p. 713
24.	November 2nd	p. 713b
25.	November 8th	p. 717
26.	November 9th	p. 717b
27.	November 12th	p. 721
28.	November 13th	p. 721b
29.	November 15th	p. 725
30.	November 16th	p. 725b
31.	November 17th	p. 729
32.	November 20th	p. 729b
33.	November 21th	p. 733
34.	November 23rd	p. 733b
35.	November 21st	p. 737
36.	November 23rd	p. 737b
37.	November 26th	p. 741
38.	November 27th	p. 741b, p. 745
39.	November 28th	p. 745b
40.	November 29th	p. 749
41.	November 30th	p. 749b
42.	December 3rd	p. 753
43.	December 4th	p. 753b
44.	December 5th	p. 757
45.	December 8th	p. 757b
46.	December 9th	p.761,p. 761b, p765
47.	December 10th	p. 765b, p. 769
48.	December 12th	p. 769b, p. 773
49.	December 13th	p. 773b
50.	December 14th	p. 777

	Enumeration Calendar	1850 Slave Schedule
51.	December 16th	p. 777b, p. 781
52.	December 17th	p. 781b, p. 785
53.	December 18th	p. 785, p. 789
54.	December 19th	p. 792
55.	December 21th	p. 793
56.	December 24th	p. 796, p. 797

Note- At the bottom of page 777b of the 1850 Slave Schedule, there are one or two names that are not legible. If a question mark (?) appears in a cell, it indicates that the record is not legible for that particular cell. I have deciphered and transcribed the information as best I could.

A key person in the business of enslavement was R. L. Watts, a Negro trader living in the Eastern District of Amherst County in 1850.

Source Citation: R.L.Watts; p.79B, family 115, Eastern District, Amherst County, Virginia Census of population; (National Archives Microfilm Publication M432, roll 933); Seventh Census of the United States, 1850; Record of the Bureau of the Census, Record Group 29.

Virginia 1850   Index to the Amherst County Slave Schedule

	Slave Owner	S	M	F	B	Mu	X	Page#
1	Ambler, Phillip St. Geo.	48	12	36	47	1		733
2	Ambler, Phillip St. Geo.	30			30			737
3	Anderson, Wm. T.	21	12	9	20	1		741
4	Appling, David	14	4	10	8	6		705b
5	Bailey, Daniel E.	16	7	9	11	5		673b
6	Barnes, Frances K.	14	5	9	14			657
7	Barrett, John Y.	15	7	8	8	7		673b
8	Bell, Thomas G.	7	4	3	7			717b
9	Bennett, Calvin	7		5	7		2	733b
10	Bennett, James	7	1	4	6		3	733b
11	Bennett, James	2	2		2			737b
12	Berry, M. S.	1		1	1			681
13	Bethel, Joel	28	14?	13?	28			785b&789
14	Bias, T.	6	1	5		6		749b
15	Bibb, Benjamin B.	7	5	2	7			669
16	Bibb, Robert C.	2	1	1	2			661
17	Blair, Frances A.	4	1	3	4			721
18	Blair, Nancy	4	2	2	4			721
19	Blanks, Dicen	5	3	2	4	1		725b
20	Bowhorne, Abner	8	7	1	8			781&781b
21	Bowles, Sarah	13	6	7	7	6		661&661b
22	Bowlin, William	15	6	9	15			785
23	Broaddus, John W.	5	3	2	4	1		661b
24	Broadus, Robert T.	6	3	3	4	2		697b
25	Brockman, Sims.	10	5	5	10			705
26	Brown Jr., Benjamin	15	7	8	14	1		709b
27	Brown, Charles S.	8	6	2	8			677b

Virginia 1850   Index to the Amherst County Slave Schedule

	Slave Owner	S	M	F	B	Mu	X	Page#
28	Brown, Fielding	4	1	3	3	1		721b
29	Brown, Joseph	1		1	1			665
30	Brown, Mathew	13	5	8	13			721b
31	Brown, Mary H.	1		1		1		741b
32	Brown, Robert M.	8	3	5	4	4		761b
33	Burford, Ambrose	8	4	4		8		661
34	Burford, George	1		1	1			677b
35	Burford, Sylvester S.	16	7	9	15	1		745
36	Burford, Wm.	11	7	4	11			685b
37	Burford, William A.	4	1	3	4			669b
38	Burks, Charles M.	3		3	3			656
39	Burks, D. J.	1	1		1			673
40	Burks, George M.	13	8	5	13			657b
41	Burks, John	1		1	1			656
42	Burks, Nancy	5	3	2	5			681
43	Burks, Rowlin P.	4		2	4		2	733b
44	Burks, Urich	2	1	1	2			709
45	Burley, William	2	1	1	2			661
46	Cabell, Mary B.	23	12	11	18	5		761b&765
47	Cabell, Mays	14	10	4	14			733b
48	Camden, Beauford	1	1		1			685b
49	Camden, Benjamin	26	15	11	26			713
50	Camden, John S.	10	6	4	9	1		713
51	Camdon, Benjamin	9	6	3	9			705
52	Camm, Elizabeth	10	5	5	10			741
53	Campbell, Benjamin	3	2	1	3			713&713b

Virginia 1850   Index to the Amherst County Slave Schedule

	Slave Owner	S	M	F	B	Mu	X	Page#
54	Campbell, Cattel	1	1		1			657b
55	Campbell, Eldridge	1		1	1			713b
56	Campbell, Eliza.	4	2	2	4			709b
57	Campbell, George H.	1		1	1			713
58	Campbell, Joshua	4		4	4			713b
59	Campbell, Lewis	6	4	2	6			773
60	Campbell, Lewis S.	20	11	9	20			785b
61	Carden, John	21	12	9	21			729
62	Carpenter, Austin	4	3	1	4			693
63	Carpenter, John	3	3		3			661b
64	Carter, Edward	2		2	2			677
65	Carter, Geo. W.	12	7	5	11	1		697
66	Carter, Joseph R.	2		2	2			689b
67	Carter, Peter	3	1	2	3			677
68	Carter, Robert	21	14	7	20	1		657b&661
69	Cash, Barnet	8	1	7	6	2		709b
70	Cash, Jas. T.	4	3	1	4			713b
71	Cash, John W.	12	4	8	12			709
72	Cash, Lewellen	12	4	8	11	1		685
73	Cash, Saml. G.	21	9	12	16	5		709b
74	Cash, Saml. G.	4	3	1	4			705
75	Chewning, Albert G.	11	7	4	11			705
76	Childress, Benj. W.	10	5	5	10			789b
77	Childress, Mary,	16	8	8	6	10		717&717b
78	Chiles, Tarlton W.	9	8	1	9			745

11

Virginia 1850   Index to the Amherst County Slave Schedule

	Slave Owner	S	M	F	B	Mu	X	Page#
79	Christian, Charles	1		1	1			697
80	Christian, Edmund	3		3	2	1		737b
81	Christian, Frances A.	29	7?	13?	29			785b
82	Christian, Mary	11	4	7	11			737b
83	Christian, Paul	3	1	2	3			689
84	Claiborn, Wm.	13	9	4	13			701b
85	Claiborn, Wm. J.	8	3	5	8			701b
86	Claiborne, Chs. B.	48	25	23	36	12		749b&753
87	Claiborne, Wm. S.	9	3	6	9			713b
88	Clark, N. L.	1	1		1			741
89	Clarke, Milly	9	8	1	9			741b
90	Cobb, Jas. N. B.	5	2	3	3	2		713b
91	Coffe, Henry	4	2	2	2	2		661b
92	Coghill, Ro. A.	29	10	19	29			725b
93	Coleman, James	26	12	14	20	6		757
94	Coleman, John	19	12	7	9		1	701b
95	Coleman, Joseph	6	4	2	6			689b
96	Coleman, Linsey	26	7	19	26			665b
97	Coleman, William E.	14	8	6	12	2		665b
98	Cox, Archa	8	4	4	8			749
99	Cox, Spotswood H.	5	2	3	5			741
100	Cox, Wiatt	24	14	10	24			745&745b
101	Cox, Wm.	3		3	3			717b
102	Curl, George G.	41	34	7	41			773
103	Daniel Jr.,Leo	7	4	3	3	4		773b
104	Davenport, Mary	6	3	3	5	1		721
105	Davidson, Micajah	2	1	1	2			721b

Virginia 1850   Index to the Amherst County Slave Schedule

	Slave Owner	S	M	F	B	Mu	X	Page#
106	Davies, Arthur B.	22	7	15	12	10		681&681b
107	Davis, E. L.	2	2		2			665
108	Davis, Ed. J.	2	1	1	2			657
109	Davies, Elizabeth	16	10	6	16			665
110	Davis, H. L.	20	9	11	16	4		665&665b
111	Davis, James B.	4	2	2	3	1		669b
112	Davis, Nancy	9	1	8	9			673
113	Davies, Sally D.	28	9	19	21	7		677&677b
114	Davis, Sarah W.	10	5	5	10			781b&785
115	Davis, Whiting	6	2	4	6			725
116	Davis, William M.	2	1	1	2			657b
117	Dawson, Mildred	10	6	4	10			673
118	Dawson, Mildred	9	5	4	3	6		657b
119	Day, Daniel	17	9	8	17			777b
120	Demsey, Wm. M.	3		3	2	1		725
121	Dillard, Elizabeth	14	5	9	14			777
122	Dillard, John	44	26	18	40	4		777&777b
123	Dillard, John J.	11	4	7	9	2		757b
124	Dillard, Terisha. W.	17	8	7	15	1		757
125	Dillard, Wm.	32	15?	10?	22	1		753b
126	Drumheller, Jno. A.	1	1			1		773b
127	Drummond, Henly	3	1	2	2	1		661b
128	Drummond, Newton	2		2	2			681
129	Drummond, Za	15	6	9	15			656
130	Duncan, Wesley S.	4	2	2	4			657b
131	Earley, John W.	3	2	1	3			721b
132	Echols, Paschal T.	1	1		1			773

Virginia 1850 Index to the Amherst County Slave Schedule

	Slave Owner	S	M	F	B	Mu	X	Page#
133	Edds, John	7	7		7			733
134	Edwards, Thomas	12	7	5	12			789
135	Ellis, Charles	19	6	13	8	11		677
136	Ellis, Margaret	6	2	4	6			677b
137	Eubank, Catherine	11	5	6	9	2		673
138	Eubank, Charles R.	6	5	1	6			673
139	Eubank, James	1		1	1			665
140	Eubank, Thomas N.	7	3	4	7			705b
141	Eubanks, John B.	2	1	1	2			669b
142	Ewers, Abram	2	1	1	2			713b
143	Ewers, Joseph	5	3	2	4	1		709
144	Fair, Wm. L.	2	1	1	2			749b
145	Faulconer, John M.	1		1	1			725b
146	Faulconer, S. M.	2	1	1		2		773b
147	Ferguson, Samuel	2		2	2			705
148	Fletcher, E.	105	33	55	61	39		795&795b
149	Fletcher, Sidney	28	15	13	19	9		717b
150	Flood, Martha	6	4	2	6			656
151	Flood, Peter	9		9	3	6		656&657
152	Fogus, Andrew	14	6	8	14			789b
153	Fonkhowitger, J. N.	1		1	1			713b
154	Fowler, Wm. O.	2		2		2		749b
155	Franklin, Henry	1		1	1			685b
156	Franklin, Jeremiah	6	2	4	6			665
157	Franklin, William	3	1	2	3			665
158	Frazier, Campbell	2		2		2		713b

Virginia 1850   Index to the Amherst County Slave Schedule

	Slave Owner	S	M	F	B	Mu	X	Page#
159	Frazier, Thos.	1		1	1			713b
160	Fugue, John H.	5	3	2	4	1		677b
161	Fulcher, Sally	2		2	2			717
162	Fulcher, Wm. H.	2		2	1	1		717
163	Fultz, James M.	2	1	1	2			721
164	Ganaway, Albert	11	4	7	11			717
165	Ganaway, James	5	2	3	2	3		705
166	Garland, James P.	13	7	6	4	9		697b
167	Garland, Saml. M.	14	6	8	12	2		761b
168	Garvin, Jas.	2	1	1	2			745
169	Gatewood, Wiat.	1	1		1			665
170	Gilbert, Wm.	13	5	8	13			781b
171	Gilbert, Z.	11	5	6	11			681b
172	Gill, C.	1		1		1		697
173	Gillaspie, Willis	3		3		3		677b
174	Gillespie, G.	1	1		1			777b
175	Gilliam, James	5	3	2	5			677
176	Gooch, Albert G.	4	1	3	1	3		657
177	Gooch, John M.	4	3	1	4			673b
178	Goode, Joseph	1		1	1			705
179	Goode, M.W.	8	5	3	3	5		757b
180	Goodrich, Ann	6	4	2	3	3		693
181	Goodwin, James	6	3	3	6			781
182	Goodwin, John L.	14	5	9	14			781
183	Goodwin, M.C.	10	6	4	6	4		657b
184	Goodwin, Thomas C.	11	5	6	11			681b&685
185	Grant, L.	3	1	2	2	1		665
186	Hall, Archa	6	2	4	6			725
187	Hanowhals	9	9		8	1		669b

Virginia 1850   Index to the Amherst County Slave Schedule

	Slave Owner	S	M	F	B	Mu	X	Page#
188	Hansand, Judith	10	5	5	9	1		661
189	Harding, Wm. O.	24	15	9	24			729b
190	Hargrove, Ro. R.	4	3	1	2	2		697b
191	Harlow, John S.	4	2	2	1	3		781b
192	Harrison, A. C.	10	4	6	6	4		773b
193	Harrison, John C.	3	2	1	3			689
194	Harrison, John R.	3	2	1	3			689
195	Harrison, Lewis	8	4	4	1	7		737b
196	Haydon, Abner	1		1	1			661b
197	Haydon, Jarvis	1		1	1			737b
198	Heiskill, Saml.	12	9	3	12			789b
199	Henderson, Richard	2	0	2	1	1		741b
200	Henly, Mary A. S.	8	3	5	7	1		669
201	Higginbotham, Absalom.	26	12	14	21	5		693
202	Higginbotham, Geo. W.	15	6	9	15			693
203	Higginbotham, James	13	6	7	6	7		689
204	Higginbotham, James	17	11	6	2	15		769
205	Higginbotham, Rufus	8	5	3	4	4		661b
206	Hill, Dabney	1		1	1			717
207	Hill, Nancy	3	2	1	3			781b
208	Hite, J. J.	15	8	7	13	2	1	656
209	Hite, James	14	7	7	13	1		685b
210	Hix, Bluford	7	1	6	1	6		657
211	Hix, Jno.	2		2	2			777
212	Hix, Mary	1		1	1			661

Virginia 1850 Index to the Amherst County Slave Schedule

	Slave Owner	S	M	F	B	Mu	X	Page#
213	Hix, Nelson	2	1	1	2			657
214	Hix, Nicholas	3	1	2	3			725
215	Hix, Preston	1	1		1			657
216	Hix, Wm.	20	13	7	16	4		709&709b
217	Hopkins, Edward P.	9	4	5	9			725
218	Howe, Elizabeth	4	1	3	4			773
219	Huckstess, Lucy	1		1	1			729
220	Hudson, Edmund	1	1		1			705b
221	Hudson, Martha A.	6	2	4	6			701b
222	Hudson, Permelia	8	2	6	7	1		705b
223	Hudson, Shelton	1		1	1			705b
224	Hudson, Wm. W.	3	1	2	3			705b
225	Hughs, Thacker	14	8	6	14			781b
226	Huntley, Joseph O.	2	1	1	1	1		673
227	Hutcheson, Thos.	10	3	7	10			785
228	Hylton, George.	5	3	2	4	1		705b&709
229	Irvine, John R.	23	10	13	23			685&685b
230	Isbell, Wm. J.	12	3	9	12			749
231	Jarvis, James	1	1		1			661b
232	Jeffries, Enoch	9		1	8	8	1	665b
233	Jennings, Daniel	1		1	1			773b
234	Jennings, Henry	1	1		1			785b
235	Jennings, J. W.	6	3	3	6			773b
236	Jennings, Powhatan	6	5	1	6			785
237	Johnson, Alexander C.	19	9	10	17	2		677b
238	Johnson, Calvin M.	2	1	1	2			725b

Virginia 1850   Index to the Amherst County Slave Schedule

	Slave Owner	S	M	F	B	Mu	X	Page#
239	Joiner, James H.	2	2		2			**657b**
240	Joiner, Peter G.	13	9	4	13			**781b**
241	Jones, Benjamin H.	12	3	9	8	4		**789**
242	Jones, Chas. H.	1	0	1	1			**792**
243	Jones, Linsey M.	4	1	3	4			**661b**
244	Jones, Sophia A.	10	2	8	10			**673**
245	Jones, Tandy	15	9	6	15			**709**
246	Jones, Thos.	11	6	5	11			**745**
247	Jones, Thos. H.	1		1	1			**789b**
248	Jones, Thos. W.	14	4	10	14			**741b**
249	Jones, Warner	3	1	2	3			**713b**
250	Jordan, Wm.	20	11	9	16	4		**749b&753**
251	Keaton, James A.	1		1	1			**705b**
252	Keith, Jas. W.	16	7	9	16			**757b**
253	Keith, Sarah	13	10	3	11	2		**757**
254	Kelly, Jesse	1	1			1		**729b**
255	Kidds, Wilson P.	6	2	4	5	1		**773b**
256	Knight, Richard	2	1	1	2			**689**
257	Knight, Sophia	6	4	2	6			**693&693b**
258	Knight, Wm.	9	6	3	9			**689b**
259	Kyle, Heram C.	10	4	6	10			**785**
260	Kyle, Joseph	10	7	3	9	1		**721**
261	Lampkin, Jas. L.	14	4	10	14			**769**
262	Landrum, Rich	6	1	5	3	3		**689**
263	Lavender, William	1	1			1		**661**
264	Lawrence, E. D.	5	1	3	5		1	**713b**
265	Layne, Elizabeth	7	4	3	6	1		**705b**
266	Layne, G.C.	3	2	1	3			**685b**
267	Layne, Thomas	1		1	1			**657b**

Virginia 1850   Index to the Amherst County Slave Schedule

	Slave Owner	S	M	F	B	Mu	X	Page#
268	Lee, James	17	3	14	17			781
269	Lee, Thos.	8	7	1	8			781b
270	Logan, William	9	4	5	9			669
271	London, Lee	8	5	3	8			789b
272	London, Nelson	2		2	2			789b
273	Long, Armstead	19		8	19			741b
274	Love, Thos.	12	8	4	11			745
275	Loving, Henry	6	4	2	6			669
276	Lyon, John N.	3	2	1	3			785b
277	Mahone, John	8	5	3	8			749
278	Malick, James B.	5	3	2	4	1		669b
279	Mantiply, N.	5	2	3	3	2		761b
280	Mantiply, Saml.	50	26	24	24	26		765&765b
281	Mantiply, Saml. & Wm.	23	11	12	23			687
282	Mantiply, Wm.	23	10	13	15	8		765
283	Mantiply, Winston	10	6	4	9	1		681b
284	Markham, George	15	6	9	9	6		665b
285	Martin, A. B.	2		2	2			697
286	Martin, Geo. H.	1		1	1			725b
287	Martin, Howard	17	8	9	17			725
288	Martin, James T.	5	5		5			656
289	Martin, R. C.	3	2	1	3			777b
290	Massie, Charles	22	11	11	22			685
291	Massie, Charles H.	9	3	6	5	4		657
292	Massie Jr., John	7	5	2	7			717
293	Mays, George S.	22	11	11	22			753b
294	Mays, Shepherd H.	4	2	2		4		689
295	McDaniel, James	12	8	4	6	6		661b
296	McDaniel, Lindsey	5	2	3	5		1	709

19

Virginia 1850   Index to the Amherst County Slave Schedule

	Slave Owner	S	M	F	B	Mu	X	Page#
297	McDaniel, William	23	12	11	16	7		665
298	McDaniel, William H.	4	3	1	4			681b
299	McDonald, Jas.	7	1	4	7		2	717
300	Mcfall, Sampson	3	2	1	1	2		677b
301	McGinns, Hiram	1		1	1			717
302	McGroover, A. B.	32	13	19	30	2		749
303	McIrver, Christopher	17	10	7	17			737b&741
304	McTinsley, George	1		1	1			657b
305	Miller, Sheffey	26	18	8	23			737
306	Miller, William S.	1		1		1		685
307	Mitchell, Pleasant	3	1	2	3			661
308	Mitchell, Powhaton	9	4	5	2	7		677
309	Mitchell, Topsley	6	2	4	6			729b
310	Mohone, Manson	6	2	4	6			785&785b
311	Morgan, Damie G.	2		2	2			745b
312	Morris, Bluford	3	2	1	3			685b
313	Morris, Elizabeth	8	5	3	8			681
314	Morris, Moses	2	1	1	2			737b
315	Morris, Randolph	2	2		2			661b
316	Morris, Rich. G.	80	43	37	80			765b&769
317	Morris, William C.	9	2	7	8	1		657b
318	Morris, William P.	19	10	9	18	1		657
319	Mosby, John A.	7	3	4	7			769b&773
320	Mundy, Alex	31	25	6	31			773b&777
321	Mundy, Jesse	47	25	18	33	6		769b

	Slave Owner	S	M	F	B	Mu	X	Page#
322	Mundy, Mary	7	4	3	7			785b
323	Myers, John	5	2	3	5			656
324	Myers, William	2		2	2			681
325	Newcomb, William P.	3	1	2	1	2		657b
326	Noel, Simon	11	6	5	11			777b
327	North, Jas.	5						773b
328	North, Richard	11	5	6	5	6		685b
329	Ogden, Agnes	11	5	6	11			737b
330	Ogden, Allison	13	8	5	10	3		753b
331	Ogden, James M.	1		1	1			737b
332	Ogdon, Armstead H.	6	3	3	5	1		669b
333	Ogdon, James	6	3	3	2	4		713
334	Ogdon, Walker R.	3	1	2	3			677b
335	Old, George W.	7	5	2	6	1		745b
336	Omohundeo, Ellis P.	22	6?	9?	22			777b
337	Page, Dillard H.	17	11	6	16	1		717
338	Page, Gabriel H.	1		1	1			717
339	Page, R. H.	6	3	3	4	2		693b
340	Palmer, Saml. H..	1	1		1			777b
341	Parks, Nancy	12	6	6	12		1	725
342	Parrish, C.W.	7	6	1	5	2		697&697b
343	Parrot, Wm. J.	5	1	4	3	2		713b
344	Parson, Chas.	16	7	9	16			697
345	Patterson, David	51	24	27	51			733b
346	Patterson, Sarah A.	4	2	2	3	1		677b
347	Pendleton, Ro. A.	6	3	3	6			713b
348	Penn, Charles A.	40	18	22	40			709b&713

Virginia 1850   Index to the Amherst County Slave Schedule

	Slave Owner	S	M	F	B	Mu	X	Page#
349	Penn, John	16	6	10	9	7		713
350	Perkins, Wm. B.	1	1		1			713
351	Peticolas, Mildred W.	5	2	3	4	1		709b
352	Pettit, Samuel	17	9	8	17			757
353	Pettyjohn, George N.	37	20	17	34	3		669&669b
354	Pettyjohn, James	16	1	15	11	5		661
355	Pettyjohn, Joseph	26	19	7	20	6		661
356	Pettyjohn, Wm.	26	9	17	26			785
357	Pettyjohn, Wyatt	37	22	15	32	5		745b
358	Phaup, Michel	15	8	7	15			781
359	Phillips, James	6	2	4	6			685b
360	Phillips, Moses	7	2	5	7			689b
361	Phillips, Nancy	11	5	6	11			741b
362	Pierce, Cornelius	14	8	6	14			721
363	Pierce, Sally M.	25	11	14	25			721b
364	Pleasants, Geo. T.	38	35	3	36	3		753
365	Plunket, Wm. H.	2		2	2			777b
366	Poindexter, Garland	14	9	5	14			773b
367	Poindexter, Wm. J.	1	1		1			697
368	Powell, George	3	2	1		3		729
369	Powell, James	1		1	1			725b
370	Powell, James	4	3	1	4			789b
371	Powell, Proper	16	13	3	15	1		749&749b
372	Prible, James R.	2		2	2			661b
373	Proffit, Jordan M.	7	2	5	7			697b
374	Proffit, London A.	5	2	3	5			657b
375	Pryor Jr., John	6	3	3	6			685b

Virginia 1850   Index to the Amherst County Slave Schedule

	Slave Owner	S	M	F	B	Mu	X	Page#
376	Quarles, Henry W.	6	4	2	6			753b
377	Quinn, Jordan S.	2	2		1	1		713b
378	Rahle, Saml.	1		1	1			773
379	Ray, George H.	1		1	1			681
380	Reed, James	1		1	1			681b
381	Reynolds, Archa	5	2	3	3	2		673
382	Reynolds, Isaac R.	37	25	12	37			745b&749
383	Rhyne, Austin B.	2		2	2			697b
384	Rice, Saml. B.	13	5	8	11	2		769b
385	Richeson, James	5	3	2	5			656
386	Richeson, Jesse	39	21	18	36	3		761&761b
387	Richeson, John	3	2	1	2	1		657
388	Richeson, Wm. A	29	16	13	28	1		761
389	Ridgeway, Robert	15	7	8	10	5		757b
390	Ringer, Thomas	3	2	1	2	1		697b
391	River, James & Hanawhals	9	9		8	1		669b
392	Robertson, Sarah N.	19	9	10	11	8		753b&757
393	Rose, Sarah E.	17	4	12	11	3	1	713b&717
394	Rose, Seth M.	1		1		1		697b
395	Rousey, Patrick H.	3	3		2	1		657
396	Royster, Thomas B.	12	6	6	5	7		705&705b
397	Rucker, A	4	2	2	4			689
398	Rucker, Alex M.	2		2	2			685b
399	Rucker, C. H.	6	2	4	6			656
400	Rucker, Edwin S.	25	15	10	23	2		729b
401	Rucker, Elizabeth	29	8	21	29			733
402	Rucker, James B.	2	1	1		2		709

23

Virginia 1850   Index to the Amherst County Slave Schedule

	Slave Owner	S	M	F	B	Mu	X	Page#
403	Rucker, John D. L.	8	6	2	8			729
404	Rucker, Nathan D.	12	7	5	12			677b
405	Rucker, Nathan W.	3	1	2	3			661b
406	Rucker, Peter	24	14	10	23	1		677b&681
407	Rucker, Reuben	6	3	3	6			781
408	Rucker, William B.	43	23	20	43			681b
409	Rucker, Willis	2	1	1	2			661b
410	Rutherford, Tandy	9	6	3	6	3		689
411	Sales, Alex	1		1	1			685b
412	Sales, Corneleus	30	13	17	28	2		693
413	Sales, George T.	1		1	1			665
414	Sales, Wm.	2	1	1	2			685
415	Salmons, Jesse J.	11	5	6	11			749b
416	Sandidge, Anderson	4	3	1	3	1		661b
417	Sandidge, Dadney	24	13	11	19	5		673b
418	Sandidge, Dudley	27	15	12	16	11		705
419	Sandidge, John S.	7	6	1	7			656
420	Sandidige, Lindsey	3	1	2	3			656
421	Sandidge, M. B.	1	1		1			656
422	Sandidge, Waller	2	1	1	2			665
423	Sangster, Sarah	7	3	4	7			705b
424	Scott, Roy B.	7	2	5	7			737b
425	Scott, Samuel	4	1	3	2	2		717
426	Scott, Wm.	29	25	4	29			741&741b
427	Scott,Wm. W.	19	10	9	15			741b
428	Seay, Charles J.	1		1	1			777b
429	Seay, Nelson	6	2	4	6			721b
430	Seay, Rich W.	1		1	1			705b

	Slave Owner	S	M	F	B	Mu	X	Page#
431	Shackleford, Frank B.	61	35	26	61			769&769b
432	Shaw, Daniel	6	2	4	2	4		685b
433	Shelton, Benjamin S.	4	1	3	3	1		729
434	Shelton Sr., John	29	16	13	29			729
435	Shelton, John R.	3	1	2	3			729b
436	Shelton, Ralph C.	5	2	3	5			689
437	Shelton, Richard	14	2	12	14			729
438	Shelton, Sarah C.	1		1	1			729
439	Shepherd, Ambrose M.	2	1	1	2			657
440	Shepherd, Jas. F. M.	16	9	7	16			789b&795
441	Shoemaker, Nicholas	10	5	5	9	1		705b
442	Shrader, Daniel	8	4	4	5	3		773b
443	Shuats, Joseph H.	20	19	1	17	3		669b&673
444	Simpson, Julias	13	9	4	11	2		669b
445	Simpson, Nancy	5	1	4	5			697b
446	Smith, Jacob	15	9	6	6	9		725
447	Smith, Joel	17	8	9	16	1		677
448	Smith, John	1		1	1			781b
449	Smith, Richard P.	11	4	7	11			705
450	Smith, Rob. J.	2	2		2			757b
451	Snider, Samuel	3	2	1	3			689
452	Snoot, Thos.	1		1	1			733b
453	Spearse, John	2	1	1	2			717
454	Spencer, Saml.	6	2	4	6			721
455	Staple, Samuel D.	1		1		1		689

	Slave Owner	S	M	F	B	Mu	X	Page#
456	Staple Sr., William	5	3	2	4	1		669
457	Staples, David	5	3	2	5			777b
458	Staples, George W.	1		1	1			656
459	Staples, John	1		1	1			721
460	Staples, Wm. A.	12	5	7	12			789
461	Staton, Andrew M.	3	1	2		3		665
462	Steane, Judieth A.	8	3	5	8			725b&729
463	Stephens, Richard	3		3	3			777b
464	Stinnet, Dabnay	1		1	1			685b
465	Stinnet, Seaton	1		1	1			661
466	Stinnet, William	1		1		1		661
467	Story, Pleasant	1		1	1			785
468	Stucker, John	16	9	7	16			697
469	Stumphy, Frank	1	1		1			749
470	Sutton Jr., Francis V.	17	11	6	14	3		713b
471	Sutton Sr., F. V.	5		5	5			713b
472	Taliaferro, Anderson	22	7	15	20	2		685
473	Taliaferro, Jas. F.	8	7	1	8			761
474	Taliaferro, Milly	6	4	2	6			685
475	Tapscott, D. H.	11	5	6	11			795&797
476	Taylor, Creed	9	5	4	9			749
477	Taylor, Edward	5	1	4	5			677
478	Taylor, Jas. C.	2		2	2			785
479	Taylor, James d	4	2	2	4			701
480	Taylor, Sally	11	5	6	2	9		773
481	Taylor, Thos.	3		2	2		1	717
482	Terry, Thos. R.	7	3	4	7			741

	Slave Owner	S	M	F	B	Mu	X	Page#
483	Terry, Walker	8	3	5	7	1		729b
484	Thomas, Radford	11	6	5	11			689
485	Thompson Jr., John	12	9	3	10	2		761b
486	Thompson, Wm. W.	10	5	5	10			769b
487	Thorton, James F.	3		3	2	1		681
488	Thorton, Peter P.	21	9	12	19	2		681
489	Thomas. Radford	7	4	3	7			689
490	Tinsley, Alexander	7	5	2	7			737b
491	Tinsley, David	13	7	6	11	1	1	709
492	Tinsley, Edward	15	9	6	10	5		725b
493	Tinsley, Isaac D.	3	1	2	3			701b
494	Tinsley, Joshua	3	2	1	3			737b
495	Tinsley, Martin D.	15	6	9	15			725b
496	Tinsley, Robert	25	13	10	25			737
497	Tinsley, Robert	32	17	15	26	6	1	757b
498	Tinsley, Zach	17	7	10	16	1		753
499	Toler, William B.	6	3	3	6		1	657&665
500	Tomlinson, David	4	3	1	4		1	661b
501	Townley, M. J.	2		2	2			681
502	Trenary, Robert	2		2	2			656
503	Tucker, Adaline B.	1		1	1			689b
504	Tucker, Chas.	56	25	31	53	3		693b&697
505	Tucker, Drury	6	3	3	6			717
506	Tucker, Edmund P.	40	19	21	31	9		689b
507	Tucker, Johns.	16	9	7	16			697
508	Tucker, Rowlin	1		1	1			717
509	Tucker, Wiatt	28	14	14	22	6		693b

Virginia 1850 Index to the Amherst County Slave Schedule

	Slave Owner	S	M	F	B	Mu	X	Page#
510	Tucker Jr., Wiatt	12	9	3	12			689b
511	Tucker, Wm.	33	22	11	19	13		761b
512	Tucker Jr., Wm.	7	3	4	7			689b
513	Tucker Sr., Wm.	16	7	9	8	8		697b
514	Turner, Geo. H.	1	1		1			777b
515	Turner, Jefferson B.	15	7	8	13	2		721
516	Turner, John L.	9	5	4	9			785b
517	Turner, Lucy A.	1		1	1			701b
518	Turner, Saml.	14	8	6	14			789b
519	Turner, Saml. H.	1	1		1			777b
520	Turner, Stephen	1		1	1			661
521	Turner, Wm.	18	9	9	17	1		717b
522	Turpin, William C.	2	1	1	1	1	1	657
523	Turpine, J. D.	5	3	2	4	1		665
524	Tuyman, J. L.	11	5	6	8	3		777
525	Tyler, John	1		1		1		685b
526	Tyler, Wm. H.	1		1	1			713b
527	Tyres, Martha	18	9	9	17	1		717b
528	Venerable, Rich. J.	1		1	1			669
529	Walker, Benjamin P.	10	7	3	10			785b
530	Walker, Garland	31	15	15	28	2	1	721b
531	Walker, Geo.	7	4	3	5	2		725
532	Waller, Sarah A.	42	14	28	42			795
533	Ware, Edwin M.	3	1	2	3			685b
534	Ware, John	6	1	5	6			725
535	Ware, Reuben	3	1	2	3		1	737
536	Warwick, Robert D.	114	70	44	114			701&701b

28

	Slave Owner	S	M	F	B	Mu	X	Page#
537	Warwick, Thomas	6	1	5	6			777b
538	Watson, Wilkins	22	5	17	19	3		697b
539	Watt, Frederick	3	2	1	3			705b
540	Watts, Catherine	12	6	6	10	2		729b
541	Watts, Charles M.	5	2	3	3	2		729b
542	Watts, Henry B.	1	1		1			665b
543	Watts, James D.	18	11	7	15	3		721
544	Watts, John H.	6	1	5		6		661
545	Watts, Mitchel	4	2	2	4			773
546	Watts, Robert W.	2	1	1	2			656
547	Watts, Roderick L.	3	1	2	3			657b
548	Watts, Samuel	10	5	5	10			661b
549	Watts, Wm. L.	3	2	1	3			721
550	Waugh, Nicholas	7	2	5	7			705b
551	Waugh, Pembroke	23	13	11	24			673
552	Waugh, Roderich	5	2	3	4	1		673
553	Waugh, William	1		1	1			677
554	White, Henry A.	9	5	4	9			741
555	White, Marcus L.	1	1		1			769b
556	White, Pleasant	7	3	4	6	1		725b
557	White, Willis	14	6	8	14			665b&669
558	Whitehead, Jno. C.	21	1	12	20	1		753&753b
559	Whitton, John W.	3	2	1	2	1		709b
560	Whitton, Susan	1		1	1			709b
561	Wiatt, Samuel J.	1	1		1			661b
562	Williams, Alfred W.	13	7	6	12	1		737b
563	William, George W.	5	3	2	5			669b
564	Williams, Haz.	1		1	1			681

Virginia 1850   Index to the Amherst County Slave Schedule

	Slave Owner	S	M	F	B	Mu	X	Page#
565	Williams, James B. A.	16	8	8	16			673b
566	Williams, John M.	23	14	9	23			789
567	Williams, John W.	8	5	3	8			681
568	Williams, Ro. R.	23	13	10	11	12		685b&689
569	Wills, Elias	3	1	2	3			725b
570	Wills, John D.	5	3	2	5			781
571	Wilson, John P.	24	14	10	24			669
572	Wilson, Louisiana	3	1	1	2	1	1	717
573	Wingfield, Charles	18	11	7	18			781
574	Wingfield, Nathan A.	2	1	1	2			777
575	Wingfield, Robert	12	6	6	12		1	773
576	Wingfield, Thos.	12	7	5	12			773b
577	Winn, Benjamin	11	7	4	11			677
578	Winton, Edmund	15	6	9	15			745
579	Wood, Henry D.	8	1	7	8			737b
580	Wood, Jesse	1		1	1			713b
581	Wood, Jesse Sr.	2	1	1	2			785
582	Woodroof, Elizabeth	21	6?	15?	21			781b
583	Woodroof, Pitt	6	2	4	6			661b
584	Woodroof, Wm. P.	2		2	2			705b
585	Woodroof, Winton	9	4	5	7	2		673b
586	Woodson, Judith	12	7	5	11	1	1	709
587	Wortham, Elliot	17	8	9	17			761
588	Wright, Ellis	1			1		1	717
589	Wright, Henry T.	1		1	1			709
590	Wright, Wm.	5	2	3	3	2		713
591	Wright, Wm	14	9	5	14			789b

1850-Description of Columns for Overseers

1. Column# 1- The numerical order of entries.
2. Column# 2- The Family number as it is written in the regular 1850 Amherst County census microfilm.
3. Column#3- The entries of surnames for overseers.
4. Column# 4- The page numbers stamped in the upper right corner of the regular 1850 census records.

Note- These entries are of those who were overseers or overseeing at the time this census was recorded. Keep in mind that the spelling of surnames vary from the actual census record to the 1850 Amherst County published index of the Accelerated indexing system, Inc. 1976. I found that some surnames were not in alphabetical order in this published index to the regular census.

1

	Family#	Overseers/Overseeing	Page#
1	823	Agea, William	131
2	812	Akers, John H.	130
3	840	Barber, James	132
4	1108	Boling,John B.	153
5	270	Bowles, James	089
6	611	Bowles, Warren	115
7	745	Brown, Fielding	123
8	33	Burks, Alexander	075
9	449	Camden, Granville C.	101
10	798	Camden, John	129
11	947	Carter, Charles L.	139
12	863	Clark, John	134
13	215	Crawford, Mansfield	085
14	814	Cuningham, John R.	130
15	480	Dawson, Charles	105
16	750	Demsey, Wilson M.	125
17	919	Fulcher, James	137
18	524	Hamilton, Mathew	108
19	1087	Hill, Edmund	152
20	945	Hill, Joseph	139
21	822	Howl, Benjamin	131
22	556	Hudson, Shannon	110
23	610	Hudson, Shelton	115
24	1047	Joiner, Wm.	147
25	505	Jones, Harrison	105
26	445	Lawson, Daniel	101
27	926	Massie, Robert H.	139
28	820	Miller, Sheffy	129
29	446	Millner, Wm. L.	101
30	1106	Mitchell, Gerry	153
31	941	Mitchell, Jesse	140

	Family#	Overseers/Overseeing	Page#
32	557	Parish, Cossin	109
33	147	Pettyjohn, Ganning	082
34	818	Pettyjohn, Rich	129
35	867	Phillips, George D.	134
36	644	Robuck, Wm.	118
37	494	Rucker, Thomas H.	106
38	851	Seay, Thomas W.	133
39	591	Staples, Edward	114
40	943	Stinnett, Jas. M.	139
41	467	Stinnitt, Dabney	160
42	889	Tayler, James	136
43	639	Thomas, John J.	117
44	1	Tomlinson, James C.	073
45	748	Walker, Garland	123
46	819	Ware, Rueben	129
47	477	Watts, G. A.	103
48	539	Watts, G. A.	109
49	860	White, Henry A.	134
50	918	Woody, Allen	137
51	1100	Woody, Allen	151
52	1062	Woody, Rich C.	150
53	779	Woody, Spotswood P.	128
54	1070	Wood, Willis	150

1860-List of Slaves 100 years and older in the Amherst County slave schedule.

1-"John", 100yrs. Blackman enumerate with slave owner, *Wm. S. Claiborne*#105, on page 8.

2- "Molly", 115yrs. Black woman, enumerated with slave owner, *John T. Elles*#165, on page 3.

3- "Hannah", 105yrs. Black woman, enumerated with slave owner, *D.G. Waller*# 632, on page 45.

4- _____, unnamed Black woman, 100yrs. enumerated with slave owner, *J.M. Williams*# 671, on page 68.

5- _____, unnamed Black woman, 100yrs. enumerated with slave owner, *Sidney Fletcher*# 182, on page 39 and 40.

6- "Easter", 102yrs. Black woman, enumerated with slave owner, *Martin D. Tinsley*# 588, on page 48.

Description of 1860 Columns

1. Column#1- the numerical order of entries.
2. Column#2-the surnames of slave owners in alphabetical order.
3. Column#3-(S) indicates the number of slaves owned.
4. Column#4- (M) indicates the number of male slaves.
5. Column#5-(F) indicates the number of female slaves.
6. Column#6-(B) indicates the number of slaves considered black.
7. Column#7-(Mu) indicates the number of slaves considered mulatto.
8. Column#8- (X) represents the number of slaves who might be deaf and dumb, insane or idiotic.
9. Column#9- (SH) denotes the number of slave houses on the estate.
10. Column#10- the page reference numbers where the slave owner can be located in the original 1860 microfilm of Amherst County slave schedule.

Note- Not all slave owners owned slaves but rented, borrowed, or held them in trust for legal reasons, etc. Some free blacks and Native Americans owned family members. There are many spelling variations from the slave schedules, the 1860 regular census, to the published 1860 Amherst County, Virginia index. Check the 1860 Slave Schedule for details about column eight.

	Slave Owner	S	M	F	B	Mu	X	SH	Page
1	Adams, Jesse A.	2		2		2		1	55
2	Ambler, Ella C.	15	7	8	15				59
3	Ambler, John J.	21	12	9	14	7		6	59
4	Ambler, P.B.	18	9	9	18			12	59
5	Ambler, P. St. Geo.	89	45	44	63	26		12	60&61
6	Amonett, L. T.	19	7	12	6	13		3	67
7	Anderson, Richard	1	1		1				57
8	Anderson, Wm. T.	15	11	4	15			6	69
9	Appling, David	10	5	5	10			1	9
10	Bailey, D. E.	25	12	13	25			6	77&78
11	Barber, Jas. R.	1		1	1				59
12	Barber, Thos. A.	1	1			1		1	5
13	Barnes, Wm. H.	11	6	5	10	1		3	46
14	Barrett, J.	9	5	4	4	5		2	48
15	Bawbrone, Presella	7	4	3	7			1	66&67
16	Beanks, Dixon C.	1		1	1			1	10
17	Bennett, Calvin	19	8	11	16	3		2	65
18	Benny, M. L.	2	1	1	2				49
19	Benny, R. T.	36	13	23	1	35		2	2
20	Bethel, Wm. J.	1		1	1			1	9
21	Bibb, Bennett	1	1		1				82
22	Bibb, Ro. C.	1	1		1				50
23	Blair, F. A.	13	9	4	10	3		2	18
24	Blanks, T. C.	3	2	1	3			1	65
25	Bowles, David	1		1	1			1	30
26	Bowles, Joel	2	2		2			1	49
27	Bowles, N. R.	1		1		1		1	42
28	Bowles, P. C.	1	1			1			42
29	Broaddus, John W.	4	2	2	2	2		2	23

	Slave Owner	S	M	F	B	Mu	X	SH	Page
30	Brockman, Sims.	11	6	5	11			3	31
31	Brown, Chas. L.	11	5	6	5	6		2	49
32	Brown, Chas. W.	4	2	2	1	3		1	4
33	Brown, Fielding	2		2	2			1	6
34	Brown, Jas. S.	9	3	6	8	1			17
35	Brown, Joseph	4	2	2	4			1	34
36	Brown, Mary E.	13	9	4	12	1		3	36
37	Brown, Ro. W.	1		1	1				30
38	Brown, Robert M.	7	4	3	5	2		2	1
39	Bryant, Nicholas	1	1		1				82
40	Buck, Mary	12	5	7	11	1			4
41	Bunnett, J. N.	2	1	1	2				39
42	Burford, Ambrose. R.	8	5	3	8			1	34
43	Burford, Eliza C.	16	9	7	10	6		3	35
44	Burford, John	1	1		1				33
45	Burford, S. L.	22	13	9	15	7		4	70
46	Burford, S. M.	1		1	1				64
47	Burford, Wm. A.	4	2	2	3	1		1	49
48	Burk, Nancy	1		1	1			1	19
49	Burks, Nancy C.	7	1	6	7			1	16
50	Burks, Nancy M.	2		2	2			1	80
51	Burks, Chas. Z.	7	3	4	5	2		1	36
52	Burk, Edward A.	2		2	2			1	75
53	Burks, Jane	5	1	4	4	1		1	51
54	Burley, Elliot H.	2	1	1	1	1			17
55	Burley, James	3	1	2	3			1	79
56	Burley, Moriah	3	2	1	2	1		1	14
57	Burley, Wm. T.	2	1	1	1	1		1	15
58	Callaway, C. M.	2		2	1	1		1	68

	Slave Owner	S	M	F	B	Mu	X	SH	Page
59	Camden, Burford	3	3		2	1		1	79
60	Camden, G. C.	2	1	1	2			2	80
61	Camden, J. M.	6		6	6			3	26
62	Camden, Jackson	3	1	2	3			1	41
63	Camns, Eliza.	16	7	9	16			2	64
64	Campbell, Benj. W.	2	1	1	2			1	44
65	Campbell, Callett	1	1		1			1	35
66	Campbell, E. S.	1		1	1			1	44
67	Campbell, Eliza.	1	1		1				7
68	Campbell, Henry	6	4	2	6			1	32
69	Campbell, John P.	1		1	1				21
70	Campbell, Joshua	1		1	1				38
71	Campbell, Lawson G.	1		1	1			1	14
72	Campbell, Lewis S.	40	17	23	34	6		8	22&23
73	Campbell, Nancy	10	5	5	10			2	41
74	Campbell, Ro. W.	1		1	1			1	32
75	Campbell, S. G.	1		1	1				35
76	Campbell, Susan	4	3	1	2	2		2	11
77	Carden, John	1	1		1				48
78	Carpenter, Catherine. J.	3	2	1	1	2		1	44
79	Carter, Edward	8	3	6	5	3		1	76
80	Carter, Elisha.	7	3	4	7			1	38
81	Carter, Elizabeth	1		1	1				38
82	Carter, Ro. H.	16	10	6	15	1		2	50
83	Carter, Ro. N.	3	1	2	3				24
84	Carter, Walker S.	6	4	2	4	2		1	26
85	Cash, Cary J.	1		1	1			1	12
86	Cash, John T.	1		1	1				39

Virginia 1860 Index to the Amherst County Slave Schedule

	Slave Owner	S	M	F	B	Mu	X	SH	Page
87	Cash, John W.	13	4	9	12	1		2	20
88	Cash, Sofa	6	4	2		6		2	20
89	Cheatwood, D. B.	7	4	3	7			2	76
90	Childs, Tarlton W.	10	8	2	10			2	51
91	Childress, Benj. W.	12	3	9	7	5		2	33
92	Christian, Chas. H.	1		1	1				38
93	Christian, Drury	9	3	6	9			1	9
94	Christian, Drury J.	3	1	2	3			2	52
95	Christian, Eloria	3	1	2	3				35
96	Christian, Frncs. A.	31	21	10	31			6	57
97	Christian, John H.	1		1	1				39
98	Christian, Mary	17	8	9	6	11		4	76
99	Christian, P. H.	5	3	2	4	1		1	62
100	Christian, Paul	2	1	1	2			1	50
101	Christian, Peter T.	8	5	3	8			2	6&7
102	Christian, Stephen. W.	24	15	9	24			4	56
103	Christian, W. R.	5	4	1	5			1	9
104	Claiborne, Chas. B.	39	18	21	19	20		5	75
105	Claiborne, Wm. S.	29	16	13	25	4		8	8
106	Clarke, Wiley	9	6	3	7	2		1	34
107	Coffey, Chas. E.	1	1			1		1	15
108	Coffey, P.C.	3		3		3			43
109	Coghill, James L.	2	2		2			2	10
110	Coghill, Ro. A.	19	7	12	5	14		4	28
111	Coleman, James. P.	2	1	1	1	1			3
112	Coleman, Linsey	34	16	18	32	2		9	40
113	Coleman, Rob. L.	15	10	5	9	6		7	29
114	Coleman, Thos.	15	6	9	9	6			29&30
115	Coleman, Wm. E.	13	7	6	5	8		3	6

Virginia 1860   Index to the Amherst County Slave Schedule

	Slave Owner	S	M	F	B	Mu	X	SH	Page
116	Cox, Archebal	9	6	3	8	1		1	62
117	Cox, R. H.	13	6	7	9	4		3	45&46
118	Cox, Thos. M.	2	1	1	2			1	71
119	Crawford, A.W.F.	1	1		1				44
120	Cunninghm, Jhn. R.	5	2	3	3	2		1	62
121	Cunningham, M. R.	6	4	2	6			1	11
122	Dameron, Geo. H.	5	4	1	4	1		2	10
123	Dameron, M.	5	2	3	5			1	79
124	Dameron, Mary E.	2	2		2			1	11
125	Dameron, Zach	6	2	4	6			2	51
126	Davenport, May	5	3	2		5		1	9
127	Davies, A. B.	9	4	5	4	5		3	62
128	Davies, Chas. C.	1		1		1		1	4
129	Davies, E.	0							76
130	Davies, Eliza.	4	3	1	2	2			48
131	Davies, Geo.T.	1		1	1			1	49
132	Davies, H. E.	2		2	1	1			76
133	Davies, H. L.	15	9	6	11	4		6	18
134	Davies, J. N.	1	1		1				76
135	Davies, James B.	9	5	4	7	2			11
136	Davies, John D.	39	15	24	37	2		6	34
137	Davies, Lindsey	2	1	1	2			1	36
138	Davies, Mrs. S. M.	1		1	1				4
139	Davies, Ro. J.	12	7	5	8	4		4	42
140	Davies, Whiting	2		2	2				76
141	Davies, Wm. H.	1	1		1				36
142	Dawson, S. M.	4	2	2	2	2		1	51
143	Day, Daniel	58	29	29	54	4		8	71&72

	Slave Owner	S	M	F	B	Mu	X	SH	Page
144	Dearing, Wm. A.	14	8	6	14			4	61
145	Dillard, James.	7	4	3	6	1		3	30
146	Dillard, John J.	26	13	13	22	4		2	53&54
147	Dillard, John Q. A.	9	3	6	3	6		2	18
148	Dillard, N. S.	1	1		1				57
149	Dillard, Nancy	52	34	18	28	24		6	58&59
150	Dillard, Samuel T.	7		7	5	2		1	55&56
151	Dillard, T. W.	33	16	17	27	6			56
152	Dillard, William	32	16	16	32			6	53
153	Dodd, Geo. W.	1		1	1				24
154	Dox, H. N.	15	8	7	12	3		3	32
155	Drummond, Edmund.	3	1	2	3				15
156	Drummond, Henry	6	3	3	6			1	12
157	Drummond, Newton	4	1	3	4			1	51&52
158	Drummond, Pat. H.	8	2	6	8			3	6
159	Duncan, Wesley L.	8	5	3	7	1		1	14
160	Duprey, James. L.	11	6	5	11			1	64
161	Edward, Thomas	10	10		7	3		2	52
162	Elles, Chas. L.	10	3	7	5	5		3	10
163	Elles, Mrs. E. H.	3	2	1	3				3
164	Elles, Jariah R.	1		1	1				10
165	Elles, John T.	3	1	2	3				3
166	Ellis, Ro. N.	8	4	4	8		1	1	52
167	Ervine, John D.	1	1		1				71
168	Ervine, M. E.	2	1	1	1	1		1	66
169	Eubank, Ann E.	9	4	5	8	1		2	4
170	Eubank, Catherine	20	12	8	18	2		2	48&49
171	Eubank, Geo.	2	1	1	2				47

	Slave Owner	S	M	F	B	Mu	X	SH	Page
172	Eubank, James. F.	1		1	1				50
173	Eubank, James. & Tho.	6	3	3	6			1	47
174	Eubank, John	4	3	1	3	1		2	24
175	Eubank, John D.	1		1	1				50
176	Eubank, Rich B.	3	1	2	3			1	50
177	Eubank, Thos. A.	6	4	2	2	4		3	15
178	Ewin, Joseph	5	3	2		5		1	65
179	Ewins, Joseph	4	3	1		4		1	74
180	Fergerson, Mrs.	3	2	1	3			1	55
181	Fletcher, Edward	18	13	5	11	7		3	63&64
182	Fletcher, Sidney	74	29	45	43	31		9	39&40
183	Flood, Henry D.	18	12	6	18			3	58
184	Flood, Peter	6	2	4	5	1		3	11
185	Fogus, A. L.	13	5	8	10	3		4	17
186	Franklin, Ben.	3	2	1	3			1	47
187	Franklin, William	10	6	4	10			2	74&75
188	Frankling, J. C.	4	2	2	3	1		1	46
189	Frasier, C. S.	1		1		1			27
190	Frith, L. J.	1		1		1			2
191	Fonkhowitzer, John.	3	1	2		3			27
192	Fugua, John H.	2	1	1	1	1		1	82
193	Fulcher, Wm. H.	2	1	1	1	1		1	39
194	Gannaway, Albert	11	5	6	7	4		1	32
195	Gannaway, Jas. M.	8	4	4	5	3		2	21
196	Garland, Sam. M.	33	21	12	19	14		2	2
197	Garvin, Jas. M.	2	1	1	2			1	70
198	Gatewood, Ro.	1		1		1		1	51
199	Gatewood, Thos. B.	2	1	1	2			1	50

	Slave Owner	S	M	F	B	Mu	X	SH	Page
200	Gatewood, Wyatt	1	1		1			1	51
201	Gidson, Samuel C.	4	2	2	3	1		1	31&32
202	Gilbert, John D.	3	2	1	3			2	33
203	Gilbert, Martha R.	1	1			1		1	48
204	Gilbert, P. M. & J. D.	3	2	1	3			1	7
205	Gilbert, Wm.	7	3	4	7			1	80
206	Gilbert, Wm. W.	1		1		1		1	29
207	Gilbert, W.W. & M. R.	4	1	3	2	2			48
208	Gillespie, Wyatt	7	2	5	4	3		1	48
209	Gilliam, Ann S.	7	4	3	5	2			4
210	Gooch, Albert. G.	6	4	2	1	5		1	15
211	Gooch, J. M.	6	4	2	6			1	80
212	Goode, Joseph	1		1	1			1	44
213	Goode, Martha W.	12	6	6	9	3		4	27
214	Goodwin, M. C.	15	9	6	9	6		3	13
215	Goodwin, Thos. C.	15	9	6	15			3	25
216	Grant, Susan	1		1		1			46
218	Greiner, Annah F.	11	7	4	8	3			2
219	Grimm, Richard	11	8	3	11		1	2	30&31
220	Hall, Jas. D.	3		3	3			1	6
221	Hargrove, R. K.	6	2	4	6			1	66
222	Hargrove, Susan	11	5	6	11			1	66
223	Harlow, John S.	4	1	3		4			19
224	Harris, John L.	1		1	1			1	12
225	Harris, Samuel S.	20	14	6	19	1		4	41
226	Harrison, A. C.	13	6	7	7	6		3	1
227	Harrison, Davis D.	1	1		1			4	35
228	Harrison, John L.	6	2	4	1	5		2	13

	Slave Owner	S	M	F	B	Mu	X	SH	Page
229	Harrison, John R.	6	3	3	1	5		1	17
230	Harrison, Lewis	2	2		2			1	7
231	Harvey, John R.	1		1	1				52
232	Hawkins, Wm.	6	4	2	3	3		2	15
233	Heiskell, Samuel	12	8	4	12			3	9
234	Henderson, Rob. B.	3	1	2	3			1	17
235	Henley, James W.	7	3	4	7			2	21
236	Henley, Mary A.	7	4	3	6	1		2	14
237	Henley, Ro. L.	5	3	2	3	2		2	13
238	Henley, Thos. H.	1		1		1			21
239	Henry, Samuel H.	8	6	2	7	1		2	1
240	Higginbthm, Abslm.	39	25	14	39			5	21
241	Higginbotham, Abs.	6	5	1	6				25
242	Higginbotham, A. G. Jr.	2	1	1	2			5	20&21
243	Higginbthm, Alx. B.	6	2	4	6			1	72
245	Higginbotham, Ben.	5	3	2		5		1	18&19
246	Higginbotham, Geo. W.	16	7	9	16			3	20
247	Higginbotham, James	11	6	5	9	2		3	18
248	Higginbotham, Joseph	1	1		1			5	21
249	Higginbotham, M. P.	18	9	9	5	13		3	13
250	Higginbotham, Rufus	10	6	4	3	7		2	25

Virginia 1860   Index to the Amherst County Slave Schedule

	Slave Owner	S	M	F	B	Mu	X	SH	Page
251	Higginbotham, Will A.	4	3	1	4			1	36
252	Hills, E. J.	15	5	10	6	9		2	67
253	Hill, Thos. G.	14	8	6	10	4		2	55
254	Hill, Wm., R.	4	2	2	2	2		1	14
255	Hite, Walker M.	16	9	7	8	8		2	30
256	Hix, Bluford	3	2	1	1	2		1	11
257	Hix, Madison	2	1	1		2		1	80
258	Hix, Mary	3	1	2	3			1	10
259	Hix, Nelson	6	3	3	5	1		1	10
260	Hix, Nicholas	6	4	2	5	1		1	10
261	Hix, Wm.	19	14	5	7	12		4	5
262	Hollinsworth, Wm.	2	1	1	1	1		1	71
263	Homer, G. C.	8	4	4	8			2	77
264	Howe, Meldred	8	4	4	7	1		1	13
265	Howl, Elizabeth	2	1	1	2			1	6
266	Hucheson, Sam.	6	2	4	6			1	36
267	Hudson, Micajah	2	1	1		2		1	31
268	Hudson, Permelia	6	1	5		6			26
269	Hudson, R. M.	3	2	1	3			1	27
270	Hudson, Ro. J.	1	1		1				19
271	Hudson, Sally	2	1	1	2				31
272	Hudson, Shannon	1	1		1				74
273	Hudson, Shelton	2		2		2		2	26
274	Hudson, Wm.	5	3	2	4	1		2	31
275	Hutcheson, John J.	10	7	3	6	4		2	74
276	Hylton, Geo.	7	3	4	7			1	15
277	Irvine, John D.	1	1		1				71
278	Irvine, John R.	26	15	11	26			4	24
279	Irvine, Samuel R.	11	7	4	8	3		3	18

	Slave Owner	S	M	F	B	Mu	X	SH	Page
280	Jefferies, Enoch P.	6	2	4	6			1	15
281	Jenning, John T.	6	5	1	2	4			12
282	Jennings, Daniel W.	2		2	2			1	9
283	Jennings, Elizabeth B.	1	1			1		2	12
284	Jennings, John W.	13	6	7	10	3		2	19
285	Joiner, Sofa	2	2		2			1	9
286	Joines, Peter G.	19	15	4	15	4		1	6
287	Jones, Benj. H.	20	7	13	20			4	54
288	Jones, Beverly	8	6	2	3	5		1	43
289	Jones, Chas.	6	3	3	5	1		1	51
290	Jones, Chas. L.	8	6	2	7	1		3	37
291	Jones, Jas. L.	1	1			1			17
292	Jones, Sarah	18	10	8	17	1		3	48
293	Jones, Thos.	4	4		4				51
294	Jones, Thos. H.	2	1	1	2			1	30
295	Jones, Warner	4	2	2	2	2		1	27
296	Jordan, Mr.	17	8	9	14	3		5	44&45
297	Jordan, Wm. P.	4	2	2	4			1	52
298	Kahle, M. P.	4	3	1	2	2		1	36
299	Keith, Jas. W.	26	11	15	25	1		4	16
300	Keith, Sarah W.	5	2	3	4	1		2	45
301	Kent, John T.	16	8	8	8	8		2	12
302	Kent, William	30	18	12	30			6	57&68
303	Kent, Wm. H.	4		4	4			1	57
304	Kidd, Ro. J.	5	2	3	5			1	67
305	Knight, Sofa	6	4	2	6			2	24
306	Knight, W. L.	2	1	1	2				80
307	Knight, Wm. L.	2	2		2			1	80

	Slave Owner	S	M	F	B	Mu	X	SH	Page
308	Kyle, H. C.	16	14	2	16			3	53
309	Landrum, B. W.	1	1			1			42
310	Landrum, P. H.	2		2		2		1	42
311	Landrum, John. H. N.	5	1	4	1	4		1	51
312	Lavender, John S.	1	1		1				44
313	Lavender, Wm.	1		1	1			1	38
314	Layne, Ann	1		1	1				25
315	Layne, G. C.	2	1	1	2			1	38
316	Layne, Geo.	21	11	10	21			3	12
317	Layne, Granvel	2	2		2			1	71
318	Layne, Powhatan	3	2	1	3			1	50
319	Lebrick, Nancy	1	1		1				33
320	Lee, Thomas	14	9	5	14			2	11
321	Lee, W. A.	17	14	3	16	1		3	67&68
322	Logan, Wm.	10	5	5	10			2	14
323	Long, Armistead	14	8	6	14			3	66
324	Love, Monroe	5	3	2	5				67
325	Love, T	11	6	5	10	1		1	67
326	Loving, Henry	13	7	6	12	1	1	3	42
327	Loving, S.	1	1		1				42
328	Mabin, John R.	7	6	1	7			1	56
329	Magan, John D.	1	1		1				64
330	Manteply, Edward	3	3		3				32
331	Manteply, Wintor	14	6	8	14			4	46
332	Mantiply, Nathan'l	10	6	4	7	3		4	28
333	Mantiphy, Samuel	87	55	32	25	62		10	28&29
334	Mantiply, Wm	36	20	16	24	12		6	74
335	Massie, Charles	21	10	11	21			4	23
336	Massie, Chas.	1	1		1				41

	Slave Owner	S	M	F	B	Mu	X	SH	Page
337	Massie, Joseph H.	2	1	1	2				23
338	Martin, Abram.	6	4	2	6			2	26
339	Martin, Howard	24	13	11	21	3		3	50
340	Martin, Howard	22	12	10	21	1		3	62
341	Martin, Jas. T.	3	3		2	1		1	46
342	Martin, Jas. W.	1		1	1			1	46
343	Martin, Nancy	1		1		1			25
344	Martin, Robert C.	1	1		1			1	71
345	Mason, Saml. W.	10	3	7	9	1		2	1
346	Mathews, Edward	28	17	11	24	4		6	33
347	Mays, Anderson	3	1	2	2	1		1	40
348	Mays, Elijah	10	6	4	10			2	56
349	Mays, Geo. S.	31	15	16	23	8		6	42
350	Mays, Geo. W.	2		2	2			1	38
351	Mays, Jas. S.	10	7	3	8	2		1	30
352	Mays, Lewis	7	3	4	7			1	54
353	Mays, Nicholas	19	9	10	18	1		2	7
354	Mays, Sarah	7	5	2	7			1	55
355	McAlexander, D. R.	16	6	10	12	4	1	2	42&43
356	McDaniel, Chas. L.	2	1	1	2			1	15
357	McDaniel, Lindsey	8	3	5	6	2		1	33
358	McDaniel, Wm. H.	10	6	4	10			2	19
359	McIver, Christoph.	24	16	8	19	5		2	69
360	McKenney, W. R.	4	2	2	4			2	66
361	Miles, Thos. A.	4	3	1	4			2	5
362	Miller, Jas.	23	11	12	14	9		4	39
363	Miller, Jas. Jr.	1		1	1				17
364	Miller, Sheffey	9	4	5	9			2	32

51

Virginia 1860 Index to the Amherst County Slave Schedule

	Slave Owner	S	M	F	B	Mu	X	SH	Page
365	Millner, Jas. M.	12	7	5	9	3		3	46
366	Millner, Wm.	10	4	6	8	2		2	36
367	Miner, Lancelot	16	9	7	15	1		4	77
368	Mitchell, E. W.	3	1	2	3			2	50
369	Mitchell, Leroy	1		1	1				44
370	Mitchell, P.	9	3	6	3	6		2	77
371	Morris, Marice	7	3	5	2	5		1	65&66
372	Morris, W. C.	11	8	3	11			2	78
373	Morriss, B. P.	26	19	7	26			4	54
374	Morriss, Bluford	5	4	1	5			2	79
375	Morriss, E. W.	9	7	2	9			2	7
376	Morriss, R. G.	94	61	33				8	81&82
377	Morriss, Susan	2	1	1		2		1	11
378	Morriss, Wm. P.	30	15	15	28	2		4	11
379	Mosley, John S.	5	3	2	5			1	80
380	Mosby, Wm. H.	58	24	34	50	8		7	37
381	Moss, Robert	2		2	2			1	41
382	Mountcastle, Tamsey	7	3	4	6	1			20
383	Mundy, Alexander	33	26	7	33			6	52&53
384	Mundy, Jesse	45	23	22	45			5	71
385	Mundy, John C.	2		2	2				52
386	Mundy, Mary	7	4	3	7				33
387	Myers, John	5	2	3	5			1	23
388	Myers, John W.	2		2	2				15
389	Nelson, Susanah	2	2		2			1	55
390	Newcomb, Ro. S.	2	1	1	2			1	51
391	Noel, Mary F.	5	3	2	4	1		1	73
392	Noel, Mary J.	4	2	2	4			1	73
393	North, Dolly	1		1		1			12

Virginia 1860   Index to the Amherst County Slave Schedule

	Slave Owner	S	M	F	B	Mu	X	SH	Page
394	North, Eliza.	10	6	4	4	6		1	12
395	Norvell, Braxton	2	1	1	2			1	64
396	Norvell, Rupel	1	1		1				64
397	Ogden, Zach	3	1	2	3			1	20
398	Ogdon, A. H.	6	2	4	6			3	51
399	Ogdon, Agnes	5	3	2	5			1	40
400	Ogdon, Alison	17	9	8	17			6	13
401	Ogdon, Jas.	6	1	5	6			3	38
402	Ogdon, Jas. M.	2	1	1	2			1	40
403	Old, G. W.	8	6	2	8			1	64
404	Omohomdro, L. J.	5	4	1	4	1		2	74
405	Omohomdro, Mary	1		1	1				74
406	Page, Dillard H.	19	9	10	17	2		4	41&42
407	Page, G. H.	4	3	1		4		1	15
408	Page, Gabril	1		1	1				38
409	Parks, G. P.	3	1	2	3			1	51
410	Parks, Granville P.	2	1	1	2			1	35
411	Parks, Mary C.	2		2		2			15
412	Parr, Wm.	12	7	5	11	1		2	46
413	Payne, Samuel S.	4	2	2	4			1	44
414	Payne, Wm. B.	3	2	1		3		1	44
415	Peaks, Lee	3		3	3			1	68
416	Pendleton, Adalade	5	1	4	5				28
417	Pendleton, Jas. S.	23	7	16	18	5		5	27
418	Pendleton, Martha. A.	23	14	9	7	16		4	52
419	Pendleton, Rob. A.	16	7	9	9	7		4	1
420	Pendleton, Rob. N.	17	8	9	8	9		2	7
421	Penn, M. C.	20	8	12	6	14			31
422	Penn, Mary C.	15	6	9	10	5		6	31

53

Virginia 1860   Index to the Amherst County Slave Schedule

	Slave Owner	S	M	F	B	Mu	X	SH	Page
423	Peters, Chas. L.	1		1	1			1	12
424	Peterson, P. A.	5	3	2	5			1	79
425	Pettett, Samuel	21	12	9	9	12		2	43
426	Petticolas, M. W.	5	2	3	4	1		2	36
427	Petticolas, Phillip A.	2	2		1	1			36
428	Pettigreen, Eliza. G.	2	1	1	2			3	7
429	Pettyjohn, Chas.	4	4		4			3	33
430	Pettyjohn, J. L.	23	14	9	23			4	73&74
431	Pettyjohn, Edward	20	14	6	18	2		3	55
432	Pettyjohn, John W.	30	15	15	30			4	70
433	Pettyjohn, Joseph	42	12	30	35	7		8	80
434	Phillips, James	9	4	5	9			2	76
435	Phillips, Lindsey	4	2	2	4			1	10
436	Pierce, H. C.	2		2		2			18
437	Pierce, J. D.	9	3	6	8	1			6
438	Pierce, Sally W.	18	9	9	17	1		4	17
439	Pierce, Wm. M.	1	1		1			1	7
440	Pierce, Virginia P.	8	5	3	8				17
441	Pleasant, John W.	15	12	3	14	1		3	35&36
442	Pleasants, Geo. T.	45	27	18	39	6		5	47&48
443	Poindexter, Garland	14	8	6	14			3	69&70
444	Powell, James	1		1	1		1		3
445	Prible, Jas. R.	1		1	1			1	36
446	Proffott, Jordan M.	3		3	3			1	6
447	Pryor, Hartwell T.	2	1	1	1	1		1	51
448	Pryor, James	4	3	1	4			1	79
449	Pryor, John	1	1		1			1	51

	Slave Owner	S	M	F	B	Mu	X	SH	Page
450	Pryor, John	1	1		1				47
451	Pryor, Mary S.	4	2	2	2	2		2	47
452	Pryor, William	1		1	1				51
453	Purkins, W. B.	3	1	2	3			1	41
454	Quarles, Henry W.	6	4	2	5	1		2	4
455	Quinn, J. A.	3	1	2		3		1	29
456	Quinn, John. S.	1		1	1				29
457	Ray, Geo. W.	2	2		2			1	49
458	Ray, Martin D.	1		1		1			51
459	Reynold, Isaac R.	18	9	9	17	1		3	73
460	Reynold, J. R.	16	12	4	15	1		4	68
461	Rhoades, Edmund	3	2	1	1	2		1	25
462	Rhoads, Paschal	2	1	1	2			1	19
463	Rhoads, Reubin	4	3	1	4			1	24
464	Richeson, Jas. L.	16	7	9	10	6		2	19
465	Richeson, Jesse V.	2		2	1	1		1	18
466	Richeson, P. S.	2		2		2			19
467	Richeson, Sam`l	16	9	7	10	6		3	25
468	Richeson, William A.	43	26	17	39	4		9	75&76
469	Ridgway, Robert	10	2	8	9	1		1	66
470	Roane, Mr.	2	1	1	2				48
471	Rob.	0							32
472	Robert, Frederick	12	8	4	11	1		1	67
473	Robertson, Arthur F.	3	3			3			8
474	Robertson, S. F.	20	12	8	16	4		4	63
475	Rose, Wm. H.	19	6	13	2	17		2	27
476	Royster, Thos B.	21	11	10	9	12		2	32
477	Rucker, Alen. M.	6	1	5	6			1	46&47

	Slave Owner	S	M	F	B	Mu	X	SH	Page
478	Rucker, Ambrose	2	1	1	2			1	66
479	Rucker, Daniel H.	15	7	8	15			3	34
480	Rucker, J. D. L.	8	4	4	4	4		3	64
481	Rucker, M. C.	7	4	3	7				61
482	Rucker, N. D.	10	6	4	10			3	76
483	Rucker, V. H.	33	15	18	29	4		9	61
484	Rucker, Wm. B.	42	23	19	35	7		8	49&50
485	Rucker, Wm. G.	11	7	4	10	1		2	68
486	Ruckers, Thos. H.	1		1	1				19
487	Rutherford, Tandy	13	9	4	5	8		3	14
488	Ryan, Chas. J.	1		1		1		1	4
489	Ryan, Mrs. John	6	5	1	6				55
490	Sandidge, Christo.	3	2	1	3				41
491	Sandidge, Dabney	26	13	13	19	6		5	16
492	Sandidge, Dudley	20	16	4	18	2		4	40&41
493	Sandidge, John S.	7	4	3	3	4		1	20
494	Sandidge, M.B.	1		1		1		1	19
495	Sattle, Catherine	3	1	2	1	2		1	29
496	Saunders, Jas.	6	4	2	4	2			16
497	Scott, R. J.	8	6	2	5	3		4	64
498	Scott, Samuel	7	2	5	1	6		2	27
499	Scott, Samuel B.	13	4	9	11	2		2	38
500	Scott, Wm. P.	15	8	7	15			2	76&77
501	Scott, Wm. W.	16	7	9	17			4	70
502	Seay, Chas. J.	1		1	1			1	23
503	Shackerford, R. D.	11	3	8	10	1		2	18
504	Shelton, Benj. S.	11	7	4	10	1		2	63
505	Shelton, Edwin L.	12	4	8	8	4		3	65
506	Shelton J. J.	6	3	3	6			1	65

	Slave Owner	S	M	F	B	Mu	X	SH	Page
507	Shelton, J. P.	1		1	1				64
508	Shelton, Mary W.	11	5	6	11			1	63
509	Shelton, Ralph C.	8	5	3	8			1	69
510	Shelton, Richard	17	5	12	17			6	63
511	Shepherd, Eleanor	6	1	5	5	1		1	31
512	Shepherd, Henry	8	3	5	7	1		1	24
513	Shepherd, J. W.	5	3	2	5			1	69
514	Shepherd, Mrs.	1	1		1				47
515	Shepherd, Mary	1	1		1				80
516	Shepherd, Peter	1	1		1				24
517	Shepherd, Peter	1	1		1			1	80
518	Shepherd, Thos.	1	1		1				50
519	Shepherd, Wm.	4	2	2	4				80
520	Shrader, Daniel	2		2	2			1	78
521	Shrader, Geo. T.	4	1	3		4			3
522	Simpson, Francs. A.	4	3	1	4			1	49
523	Simpson, Julias	16	10	6	15	1		3	47
524	Simpson, N.	4	1	3		4			13
525	Simpson, Nancy	1		1	1			1	13
526	Simpson, Wm. L.	1		1	1				47
527	Simpson, Wm. T.	1	1		1				13
528	Sipon, Polly	3	3		3				1
529	Smith, Edward J.	2	1	1	2			1	10
530	Smith, Henry E.	23	15	8	18	5		8	15
531	Smith, Jacob	14	4	10	12	2		2	5&6
532	Smith, Joel F.	15	5	10	9	6		3	26
533	Smith, John W.	10	3	7	2	8		2	25
534	Smith, Joseph	2		2		2		1	25
535	Smith, Mary T.	12	6	6	12			2	31

	Slave Owner	S	M	F	B	Mu	X	SH	Page
536	Smith, Nancy E.	1	1		1				24
537	Smith, Ro. J.	4	2	2	4			1	49
538	Smith, Wm.	1		1		1			14
539	Smoot, John	1		1	1			1	7
540	Snead, Rod. W.	14	7	7	6	8		4	82
541	Spencer, Sam`l	9	5	4	5	4		1	9
542	Spillam, Jas. M.	32	23	9		2		5	72&73
543	Stanfield, Isaac O.	6	1	5	1	5		1	27
544	Stanfield, Wm. B.	3	2	1	2	1			44
545	Staple, Wm. A.	13	7	6	13			2	72
546	Staples, Francis G.	4		4	2	2		1	73
547	Staples, Jas. B.	2	1	1	2				43
548	Staples, John S.	1		1	1			1	9
549	Staples, Robert B.	4	1	3	4				21
550	Steptoe, S.	2	1	1	2				30
551	Stephen	2	1	1	2				71
552	Stephen, Elizabeth	4		4	4			1	71
553	Stephen, M.	3		3	2	1			50
554	Stinnett, C. A.	2		2		2			15
555	Stinnett, Seaton	1		1	1			1	30
556	Stinnett, Taliver	4	2	2		4		1	16
557	Story, P. N.	8	4	4	8			2	38
558	Sutphen, Mrs. M. H.	3	1	2	3			1	9
559	Swan, Rich. W.	13	7	6	11	2		1	51
560	Swann, Ro. N.	1		1	1				35
561	Taliaferro, Jas. E.	3	2	1	1	2		2	14
562	Taliaferro, Jas. F.	7	6	1	7			3	42
563	Taliaferro, Jas. M.	9	5	4	9			2	23
564	Taliaferro, John F.	7	6	1	7			1	25

	Slave Owner	S	M	F	B	Mu	X	SH	Page
565	Taliaferro, Maj. A.	25	9	16	22	3		5	26
566	Taliaferro, Rob. P.	3		3		3		1	23
567	Tapscott, D. H.	8	3	5	3	5			3
568	Taylor, Jas. C.	6	4	2	6			1	55
569	Taylor, James D.	6	6		1	5		2	1
570	Taylor, Samuel G.	3	2	1	3			1	25
571	Terry, Thomas R.	14	1	13	14			2	64
572	Terry, Walker	9	5	4	5	4		2	62
573	Terry, Wm. R.	9	4	5	6	3		2	74
574	Thomas, A. F.	16	10	6	7	9		5	24
575	Thomas, Radford	6	1	5	6			1	55
576	Thompkins, Alex.	4	3	1	3	1			48
577	Thompkins, F. O.	7	5	2	3	4		1	48
578	Thompson, John J.	5	3	2	4	1			41
579	Thompson, John Jr.	11	6	5	3	8		3	9
580	Thornton, J. F.	6	3	3	6			1	77
581	Thornton, Wm. F.	6	4	2	5	1		2	77
582	Thurston, R. H.	6	5	1	6			3	77
583	Tinsley, David	15	6	9	13	2		2	43&44
584	Tinsley, G. F.	3	1	2	2	1		1	76
585	Tinsley, Geo. M.	2		2	1	1		1	12
586	Tinsley, J. D.	5	2	3	1	4		1	65
587	Tinsley, J. T.	6	3	3	6			2	33
588	Tinsley, Martin D.	15	7	8	15			3	48
589	Tinsley, Martin D.	9	6	3	8	1		1	66
590	Tinsley, Robert	47	22	25	38	9	2	7	3
591	Tinsley, Z. D.	19	12	7	15	4	1	3	62&63
592	Toles, Wm. B.	11	6	5	11			2	36
593	Tomlinson, Edwin.	1	1		1				46

Virginia 1860   Index to the Amherst County Slave Schedule

	Slave Owner	S	M	F	B	Mu	X	SH	Page
594	Tomlinson, Thos. G.	2	1	1	2			1	16
595	Tucker, Amelia S.	3	2	1	2	1			10
596	Tucker, C.	8	2	6	7	1			8
597	Tucker, Charles	77	40	37	64	13		9	21&22
598	Tucker, Edmond P.	7	3	4	6	1		1	26
599	Tucker, G.A.R.	3	1	2	3			3	4
600	Tucker, Harry	5	3	2	5			1	21
601	Tucker, John S.	25	15	10	25			4	34&35
602	Tucker, Martha. A.	3	2	1	3				10
603	Tucker, Pamelia. M.	6	5	1	3	3		3	7&8
604	Tucker, Robert B.	3	2	1	1	2		2	8
605	Tucker, Roland	4	1	3	4			1	21
606	Tucker, Thos. J.	1	1		1				10
607	Tucker, Wm.	3	2	1	3			1	20
608	Tucker, William	27	19	8	27			4	65
609	Tucker, Wyatt	5	3	2	5			1	20
610	Tuning, A. G.	20	14	6	14	6		3	43
611	Turner, Edward	11	4	7	6	5		4	14
612	Turner, Frances	22	13	9	15	7		4	30
613	Turner, Geo. H.	3	1	2	3			1	55
614	Turner, John L.	11	6	5	7	4		2	38
615	Turner, Jefferson D.	15	5	10	15			3	17
616	Tuner, S. B.	2	2		2				77
617	Turner, Samuel D.	8	3	5	8			2	58
618	Turner, Stephen	3	2	1	2			1	48
619	Turner, Wm. S.	5	1	4	5				4
620	Turpin, J. T.	3	2	1	3			1	77

	Slave Owner	S	M	F	B	Mu	X	SH	Page
621	Turpin, Thos. E.	1		1	1			1	50
622	Turpin, Wm. C.	2	1	1	2			1	50&51
623	Tyree, Barthena	1		1	1				14
624	Tyree, Frances	2		2	2				14
625	Tyree, Jacob	5	4	1	5			1	19
626	Tyree, Lucas P.	1		1	1				14
627	Tyree, Martha	9	5	4	9			4	14
628	Walker, Benj.	14	10	4	14			3	53
629	Waller, Meredith	1		1	1				32
630	Walker, Samuel B.	20	10	10	20			5	57
631	Waller, Anah R.	7	2	5	7				45
632	Waller, D. G.	7	3	4	7			8	45
633	Waller, Jane M.	5	3	2	2	3			45
634	Waller, Martha H.	7	2	5	7				45
635	Waller, Sally G.	44	1	3	3	1			45
636	Waller, Wm. M.	9	3	6	9			2	7
637	Waller, Samuel M.	5	1	4	5				45
638	Ward, Ferrel	3	2	1	3				16
639	Ware, E.	2		2	2			1	79
640	Ware, Edwin M.	7	1	6	7			2	6
641	Ware, Reubin B.	8	4	4	8				38
642	Ware, Wilkinson. M.	1		1	1			1	38
643	Warwick, Jacob	31	11	20	24	7		6	44
644	Warwick, Thom. J.	12	9	3	11	1		3	58
645	Watson, Mrs. E.	1		1	1				26
646	Watts, A. D.	14	6	8	13	1		3	61
647	Watts, Chas. M.	10	5	5	10			2	54&55
648	Watts, Henry B.	2	1	1	1	1		1	46
649	Watts, Jas. D.	23	11	12	22	1		5	45

Virginia 1860   Index to the Amherst County Slave Schedule

	Slave Owner	S	M	F	B	Mu	X	SH	Page
650	Watts, John H.	10	4	6	1	9		2	15
651	Watts, Lawson	1	1		1				48
652	Watts, Ludwell	1		1	1			1	52
653	Watts, Mitchell	7	1	6	7			1	37
654	Watts, Samuel C.	1		1	1			1	38
655	Watts, Stephen	15	8	7	10	5		3	36&37
656	Watts, Thos. D.	3	2	1	2	1		1	46
657	Waugh, James H.	31	13	18	12	19		4	10
658	Waugh, Nicholas	5	2	3	5			1	51
659	Waugh, P. E.	101	46	55	101			6	78&79
660	Waugh, Wm.	6	4	2	6			1	76
661	Wheeler, John V.	4	2	2	4			2	9
662	White, J. H.	3		3	3			1	68
663	White, Sarah	1	1		1				23
664	White, Willis	27	13	14	27			4	19&20
665	Whitehead, Bartholomew	17	9	8	17			4	44
666	Whitehead, Thos.	8	3	5	6	2		2	3
667	Whitton, Augustus D.	3	1	2	3			1	14
668	Whitton, Joab W.	1	1		1				7
669	Willemore, W. L.	1		1	1				69
670	William, Hazael	6	4	2	6			1	49
671	William, J. M.	30	17	13	30			6	68
672	Williams, A. W.	23	13	11	19	4		5	5
673	Williams, Jas. B. L.	19	8	11	19			4	4&5
674	Williams, John	5	1	4	4	1			
675	Wilmor, Bradford. L.	2	1	1	2			1	23
676	Wills, Henry W.	7	6	1	6	1		2	4

	Slave Owner	S	M	F	B	Mu	X	SH	Page
677	Wills, John D.	5		5		5		1	73
678	Wilsher, Robert C.	3	2	1	3			2	7
679	Wilsher, Stafford. K.	2		2	2				7
680	Wilson, John P.	26	9	17	19			4	8
681	Wilson, Polly	2	1	1	1	1			43
682	WingField, Elizabeth	12	4	8	7	5	1	2	1
683	Wingfield, Sallie	10	5	5	10			2	71
684	Wingfield, Nathan. A.	2	1	1	2				52
685	Wingfield, Powhat.	3	1	2	3			1	40
686	Wingfield, Thomas	1	1		1				71
687	Winn, Mary J.	8	3	5		8		3	4
688	Winston, Edmund	5	3	2	5			1	66
689	Winston, Eliza.	7	4	3	7			1	66
690	Wright, Shelton	2	2		2			1	38
691	Wood, Henry D.	17	9	8	16	1		3	69
692	Wood, Jesse T.	1	1		1				32
693	Woodroof Ambros.	17	11	6	14	3		3	35
694	Woodroof, Lipton	6	2	4	6			1	8
695	Woodroof, M.	2		2	1	1			35
696	Woodroof, Winton	12	4	8	7	5		2	5
697	Woodson, Mathew	6	1	5	6				32
698	Woodson, W. H.	2	1	1	2				62
699	Wortham, Samuel	6	5	1	6			1	62
700	Wright, Ellen	1	1		1				41
701	Wright, Wm.	12	6	6	12			2	38

1860-Descriptions of Columns

for Overseers

1. Column# 1- the numerical order of entries.
2. Column# 2- the family number as it is written in the regular 1860 Amherst County census microfilm.
3. Column#3- the entries of surnames for overseers.
4. Column# 4- the page numbers marked at the top of the 1860 census page alternating from the right corner to the left corner.

Note- These entries are of those who were overseers or overseeing at the time this census was taken. The spelling of surnames vary from the actual census record to the 1860 Amherst County published index of the Accelerated indexing system, Inc. 1976.

	Family#	Overseers/Overseeing	Page #
1	379	Allen, Jas. M.	279
2	401	Allen, Wm.	282
3	53	Bennett, Geo.	236
4	939	Bibbs, Wm. C.	355
5	619	Bowles, Chas. W.	311
6	784	Bowles, Nathane, R.	333
7	571	Burks, Andrew J.	305
8	1303	Burk, Edward A.	405
9	1121	Burk, R. M.	380
10	80	Campbell, Jas.	239
11	441	Campbell, John P.	289
12	644	Campbell, Sam G.	314
13	1273	Carter, Charles. T.	400
14	1262	Carter, Patrick	398
15	455	Carter, Ro. N.	290
16	553	Cash, Jas. L.	303
17	337	Clements, James	273
18	448	Clements, Jesse	289
19	573	Christian, Chas. A.	306
20	783	Christian, Jas. B.	332
21	1072	Christian, John H.	372
22	782	Clarley, Wm.	332
23	776	Coffey, Meredith J.	331
24	908	Duff, Preston	351
25	973	Eugbank, Wm. E.	360
26	775	Evan, Chas.	331
27	127	Fitzgerald, James M.	244
28	1305	Grant, P. H.	405
29	526	Grant, Preston J.	299
30	670	Hamelton, Jas. S.	317

	Family#	Overseers/Overseeing	Page #
31	1001	Harden, Wm. H.	363
32	707	Henderson, J. M.	322
33	1287	Jam, Hylte ?	402
34	121	Johnson, John	243
35	437	Lawhone	288
36	461	Lawhorne, M. D.	291
37	275	M., Paulus	265
38	425	Mattew, Hamilta	286
39	521	Mays, Rob. H.	298
40	518	McDaniel, John J.	298
41	352	Miller, James Jr.	275
42	458	Mitchell, G. M.	290
43	803	Mitchell, Leroy	336
44	1056	Page. Jane	370
45	275	Page, Paulus	265
46	773	Page, Ro. J.	331
47	1008	Phelps, Chas. B.	364
48	1254	Phelps, Nelson	397
49	1266	Proffitt, Jas. M.	399
50	244	Simeon, Weakley	261
51	872	Simpson, Wm. L.	345
52	524	Staton, Andrew S.	298
53	1000	Thomas, Wm.	363
54	259	Thompson, Wm. M.	263
55	262	Tyree, Lucas	263
56	1029	Webb, Thos. S.	367
57	1018	Weekley, J. T.	365
58	1028	Weight, David	367
59	162	Wight, John	249
60	877	Wilmore, Ro.	346

	Family#	Overseers/Overseeing	Page #
61	93	Wilsher, Robert C.	240
62	287	White, Benj.	267
63	972	White, William. H.	359

Bibliography

Amherst County, Virginia, *Slave Schedules*; Page, 656-797 [handwritten, dark marker, top of page, alternating left to right]; (National Archives Microfilm Publication M432, roll 983); Slave Population of the Seventh Census of the United States, Second Series, 1850; Records of the Bureau of the Census, Record Group 29; NARA-Mid Atlantic Region (Center City Philadelphia).

Amherst County, Virginia. Population Schedules; Page, 73-154 [stamped, top of page]; (National Archives Microfilm Publication M432, roll 933); White and Free Colored Population of the Seventh Census of the United States, First Series, 1850; Records of the Bureau of the Census, RG 29; NARA-Mid Atlantic Region (Center City Philadelphia).

Amherst County, Virginia, *Slave Schedules*; Page, 1-82 [handwritten, top of page, alternating left to right]; (National Archives Microfilm Publication M653, roll 1386); Slave Population of the Eighth Census of the United States, Vol.1, 1860; Records of the Bureau of the Census, RG 29; NARA-Mid Atlantic Region (Center City Philadelphia).

Amherst County, Virginia, Population Schedule; Page, 229-424 [handwritten, top of page, dark marker]; (National Archives Microfilm Publication M653, roll 1332); White and Free Colored Population of the Eighth Census of the United States, Vol.2, 1860; Records of the Bureau of the Census, RG 29; NARA-Mid Atlantic Region (Center City Philadelphia).

Bibliography

Virginia 1850 Census Index. Accelerated Indexing System, Inc., 1976. NARA-Mid Atlantic Region (Center City Philadelphia).

Jackson, Ronald Vern, and Associates. Virginia 1860 Census Index: Accelerated Indexing Systems International, 1988. NARA-Mid Atlantic Region (Center City Philadelphia).

R.L.Watts; p.79B, family 115, Eastern District, Amherst County, Virginia Census of population; (National Archives Microfilm Publication M432, roll 933); Seventh Census of the United States, 1850; Record of the Bureau of the Census, Record Group 29.

Seventh Census of the United States 1850, Vol.1 (population), Series 12: Norman Ross Publishing Inc., 1990. Washington: Robert, Armstrong, Public Printer, 1853.

Eighth Census of the United States 1860, Vol.1 (population), Series 16: Norman Ross Publishing Inc., 1990. Washington: Government Printing office, 1864.

Sperry, Kip. Reading Early American Handwriting, 1998. Genealogical Publishing Co., Sixth printing, 2008.

www.ingramcontent.com/pod-product-compliance
Lightning Source LLC
LaVergne TN
LVHW021618080426
835510LV00019B/2633